lay FOR-meh: KO-meh see DEE-chay? (Italian)

lahss FOR-mahss: ¿KO-mo say DEE-say? (Spanish)

leh form: ko-mawnh luh deet-awnh? (French)

shapes: how do you say it? (English)

las formas: ¿como se dice?

le forme: come si dice?

Shapes:
How Do You Say It?
English · French · Spanish · Italian
by Meredith Dunham

les formes: comment le dit-on?

Lothrop, Lee & Shepard Books   New York

shapes: how do you say it?

First Edition   1   2   3   4   5   6   7   8   9   10

Library of Congress Cataloging in Publication Data
Dunham, Meredith.   Shapes: how do you say it?
English, French, Italian, and Spanish. Summary: Introduces different shapes in
illustrations and appropriate descriptive words in English, French, Spanish and Italian.
1. Geometry—Juvenile literature. [1. Shape. 2. Geometry. 3. Picture dictionary, Polyglot]
I. Title.   QA447.D86   1987   516.2'2   86-27740
ISBN 0-688-06952-5   ISBN 0-688-06953-3 (lib. bdg.)

12-22-95

To Professor E. Trautvetter in appreciation

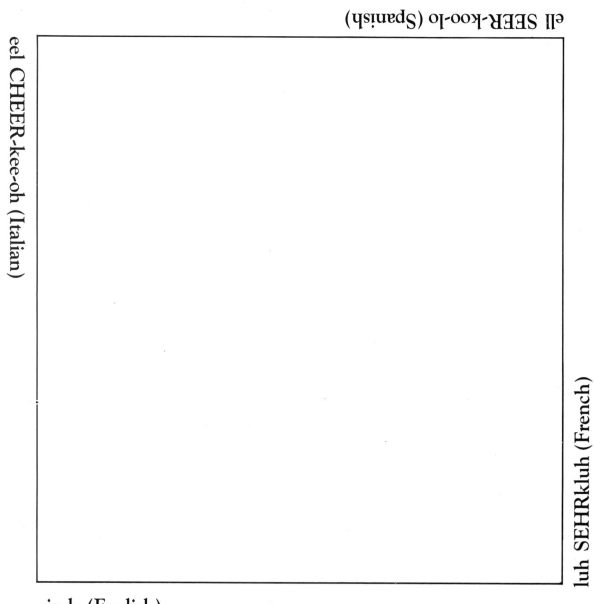

circle (English)

eel CHEER-kee-oh (Italian)

el SEER-koo-lo (Spanish)

luh SEHRkluh (French)

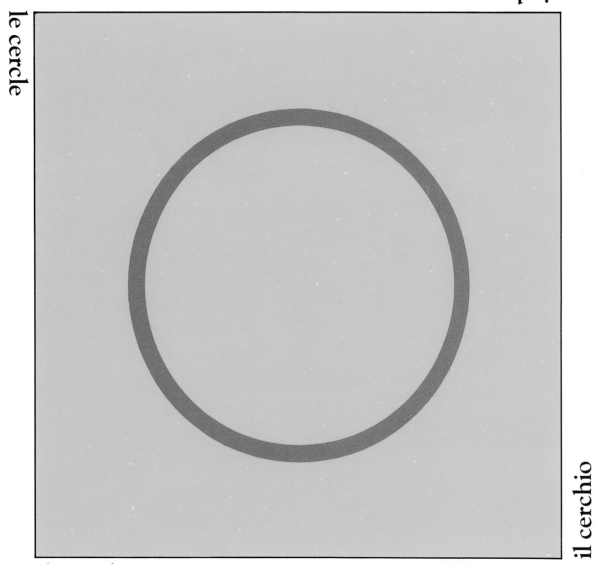

 circle

le cercle

il cerchio

el círculo

square (English)

luh kah-reh (French)

eel kwahd-RAH-toh (Italian)

ell kwah-DRAH-toh (Spanish)

square

le carré

il quadrato

el cuadrado

luh trah-pehz (French)

eel trah-PAY-tsyoh (Italian)

ell trah-PAY-see-o (Spanish)

le trapèze

il trapezio

el trapecio

oval (English)

loh-vahl (French)

loh-VAH-lay (Italian)

ell OH-vah-lo (Spanish)

oval

l'ovale

el óvalo

l'ovale

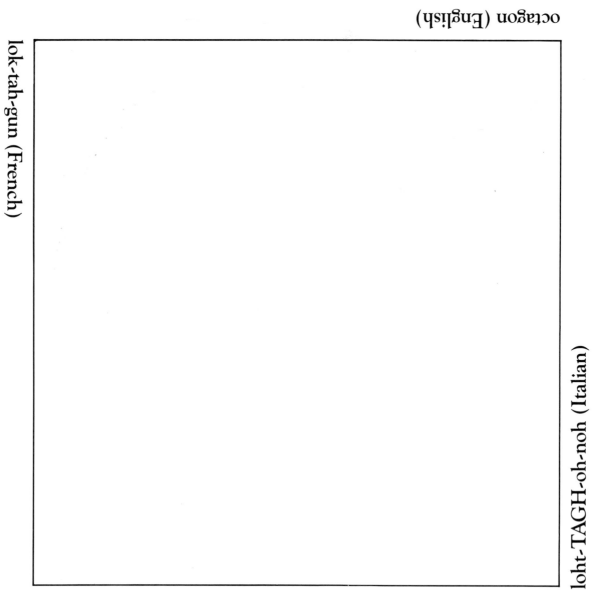

octagon (English)

lok-tah-gun (French)

loht-TAGH-oh-noh (Italian)

ell ok-TAH-go-no (Spanish)

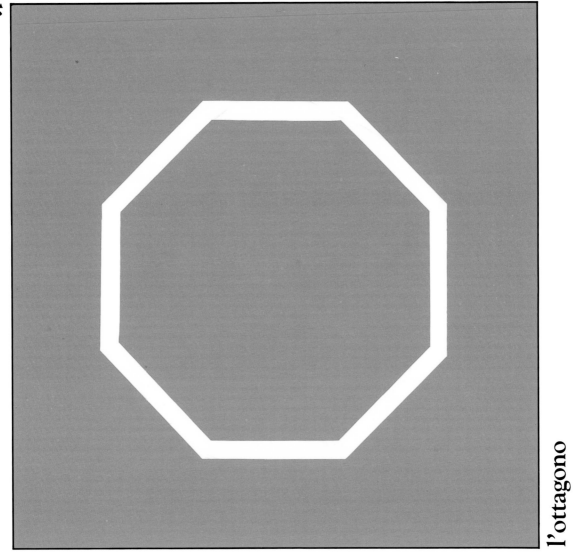

l'octagone

l'ottagono

el octágono

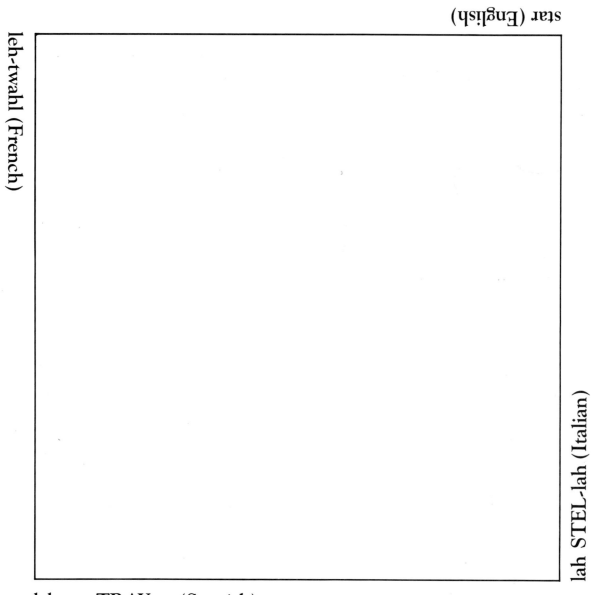

star (English)

leh-twahl (French)

lah STEL-lah (Italian)

lah ess-TRAY-ya (Spanish)

star

l'étoile

la stella

la estrella

diamond (English)

luh lo-zahnzh (French)

eel RHOM-boh (Italian)

ell ROM-bo (Spanish)

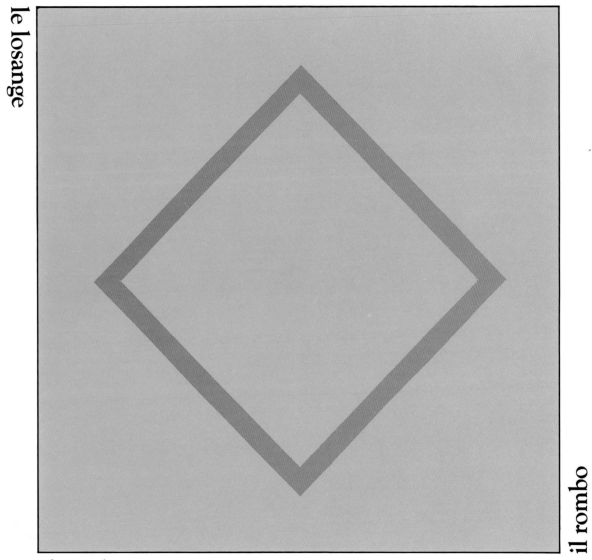

le losange

diamond

el rombo

il rombo

triangle (English)

luh TREE-AWNGGluh (French)

eel tree-ANGH-oh-lo (Italian)

ell tree-AHN-goo-lo (Spanish)

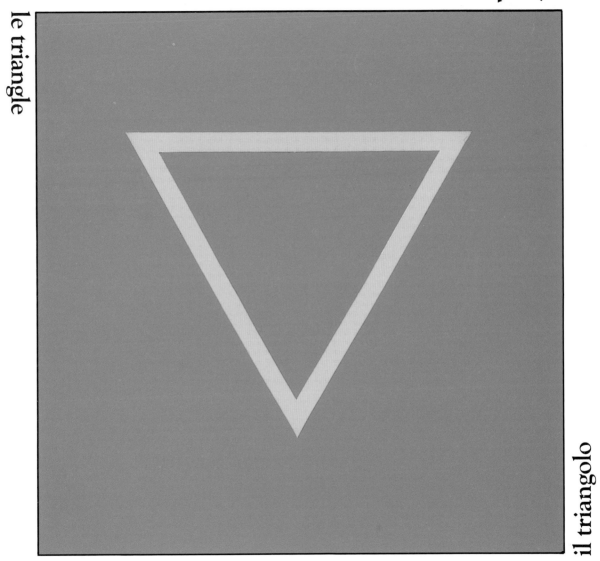

le triangle

triangle

el triángulo

il triangolo

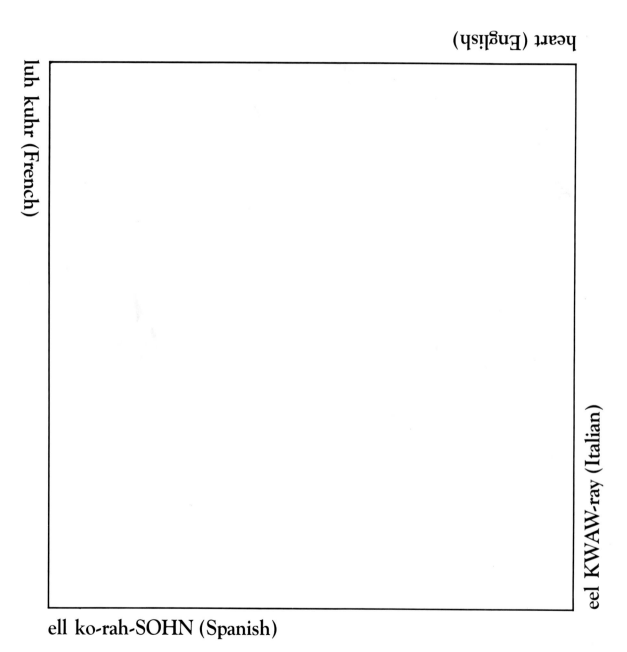

heart (English)

luh kuhr (French)

eel KWAW-ray (Italian)

ell ko-rah-SOHN (Spanish)

heart

le coeur

il cuore

el corazón

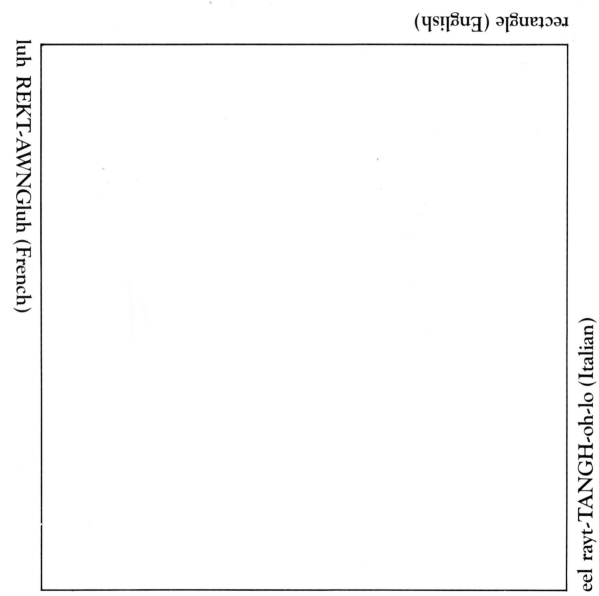

rectangle (English)

luh REKT-AWNGluh (French)

eel rayt-TANGH-oh-lo (Italian)

ell rek-TAHN-goo-lo (Spanish)

le rectangle

il rettangolo

el rectángulo

A Note on How You Say It

Read the pronunciation guides as if you were reading English text, accenting the syllables in capital letters. This will give the approximate sound of the French, Spanish, and Italian phrases. It can only be approximate because each language has some sounds that do not exist in English.

In French, the R is pronounced far back in the throat. The U (represented here as EW) is pronounced by rounding the lips for OO and saying EE instead. The nasal sound represented as a vowel plus NH (like ANH) is made by saying the vowel "through the nose."

In Spanish, the R is trilled with the tip of the tongue. A double R (RR) is trilled longer than a single R.

In Italian, the R is also trilled. A double consonant is pronounced longer than a single consonant.

Many vowel sounds in English are actually combinations of sounds. For example, if you say the word *make* slowly, you will hear EH and EE in the sound of the *a*. In French, Spanish, and Italian, the vowels are pure—containing only one sound.

If you listen to a native or trained speaker of these languages, you will notice other differences. But that's no reason not to have the fun of saying it in French, Spanish, and Italian!